createspace
www.createspace.com

© 2012 Geoffrey W. Haas. All Rights Reserved.
Illustrations copyright Louise Satterfield

No part of this book may be reproduced, stored in a retrieval system,
or transmitted by any means without the written permission of the author.

Published by createspace

ISBN-13: 978-1481083294
ISBN-10: 1481083295

Library of Congress Control Number: 2012906414

Because of the dynamic nature of the Internet, any web addresses or links contained in this book may have changed since publication and may no longer be valid. The views expressed in this work are solely those of the author and do not necessarily reflect the views of the publisher, and the publisher hereby disclaims any responsibility for them.

Summary: Pigs, ducks, mice, squirrels, lambs, rabbits, and a turtle or two all join in the fun to illustrate our changing seasons

Who Knows The Seasons?

By Geoffrey Haas

Illustrated by Louise Satterfield

Happiness is reading! Enjoy, Geoff :)

For Sara, my love - GWH

Thanks for the jump-start Geoff - LBS

Who Knows it's Spring?

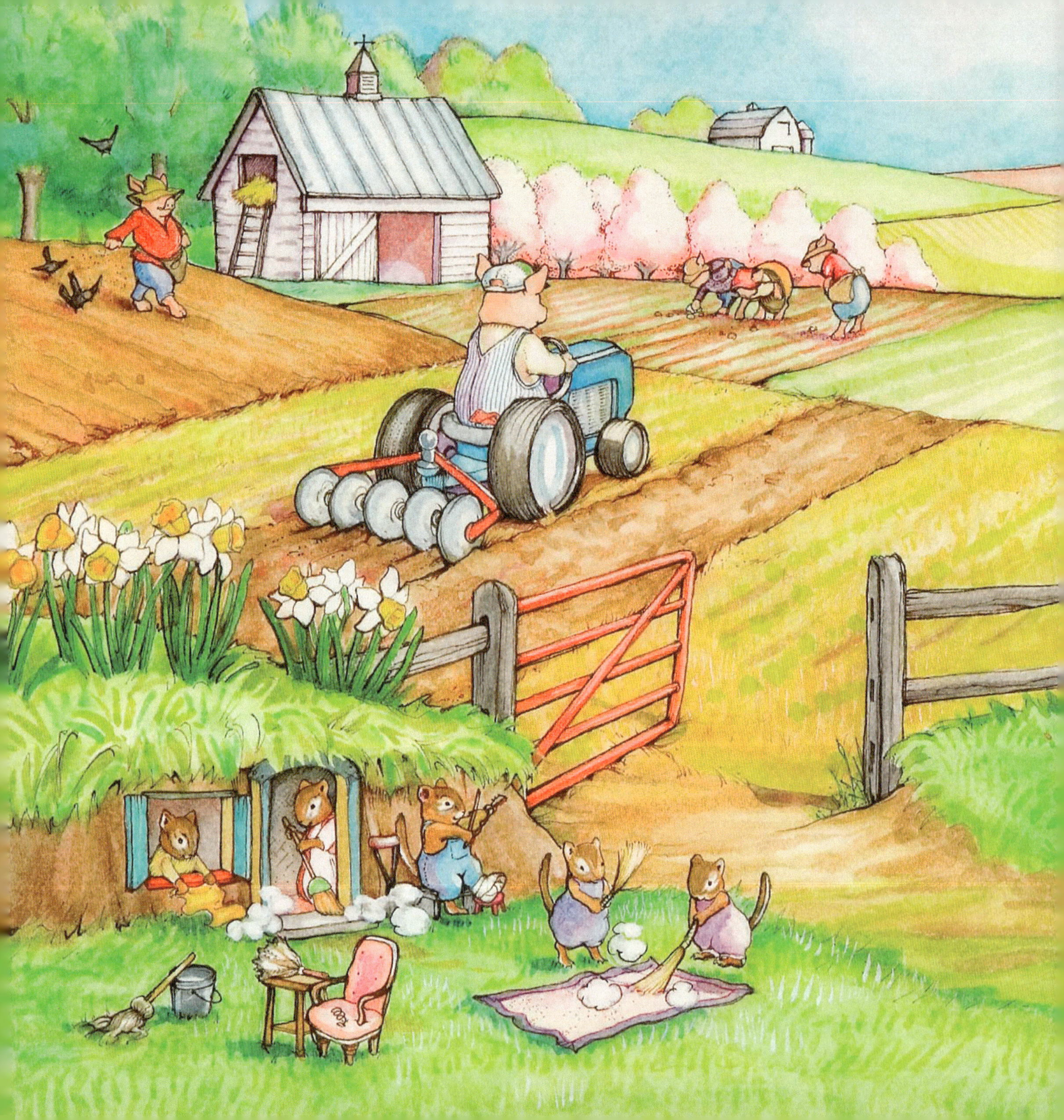

Busy farmers and bouncing lambs know it's spring.

Buzzing bumblebees know it's spring.

Splashing puddles know it's spring.

What do you like about spring?

Who Knows it's Summer?

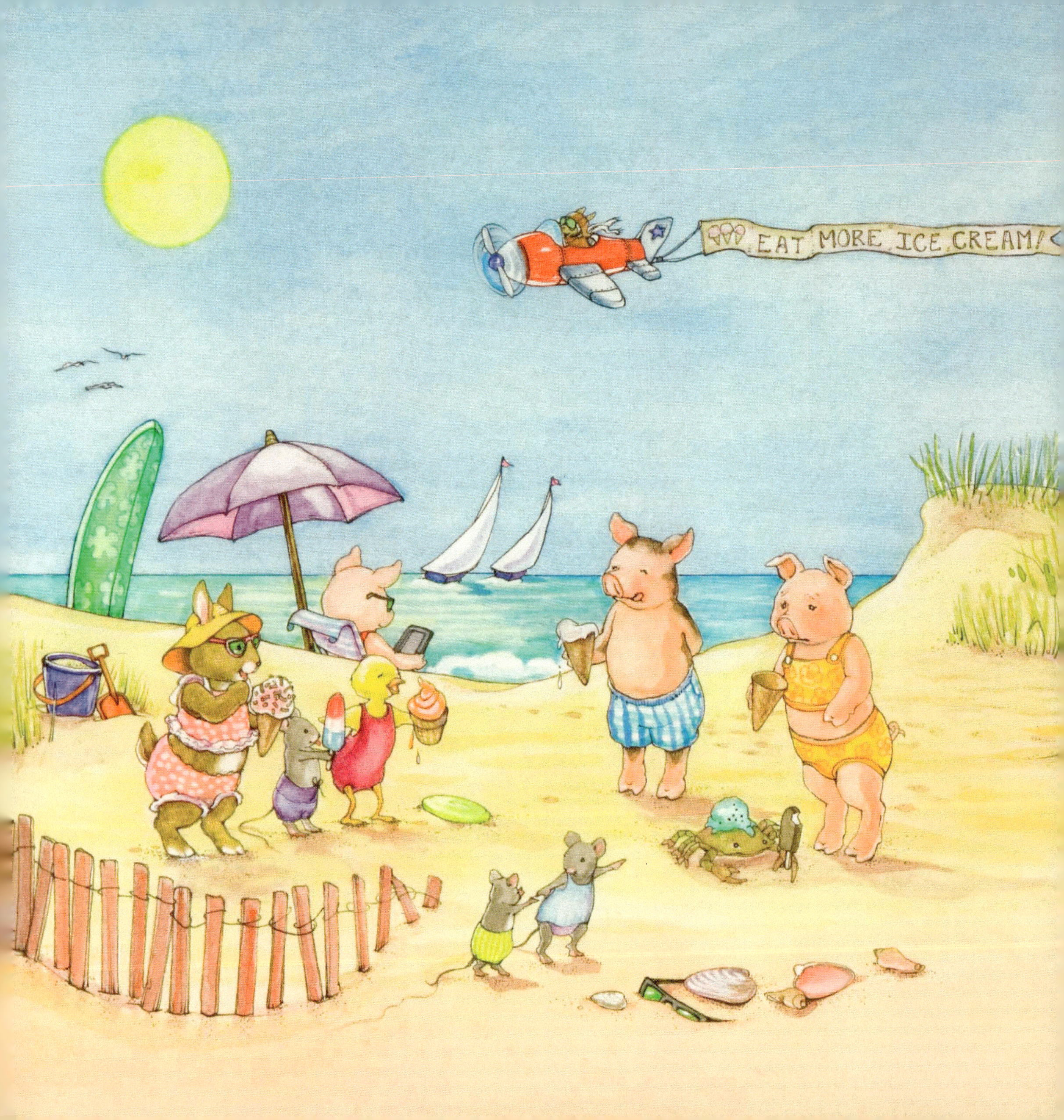
EAT MORE ICE CREAM!

Soaring kites and melting ice cream know it's summer.

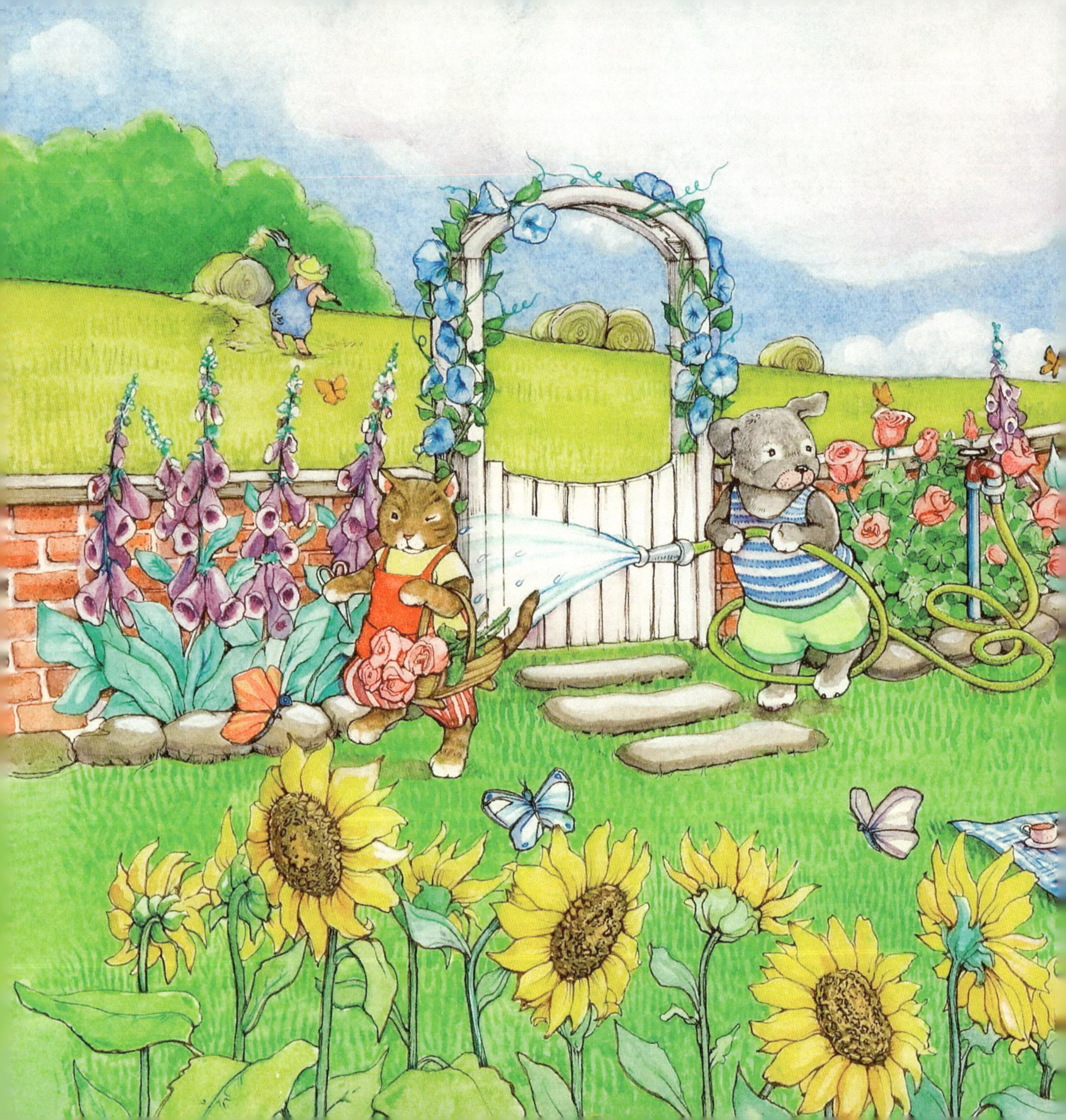

Nodding sunflowers and roaring lawnmowers know it's summer.

What do you like about summer?

Who Knows it's Fall?

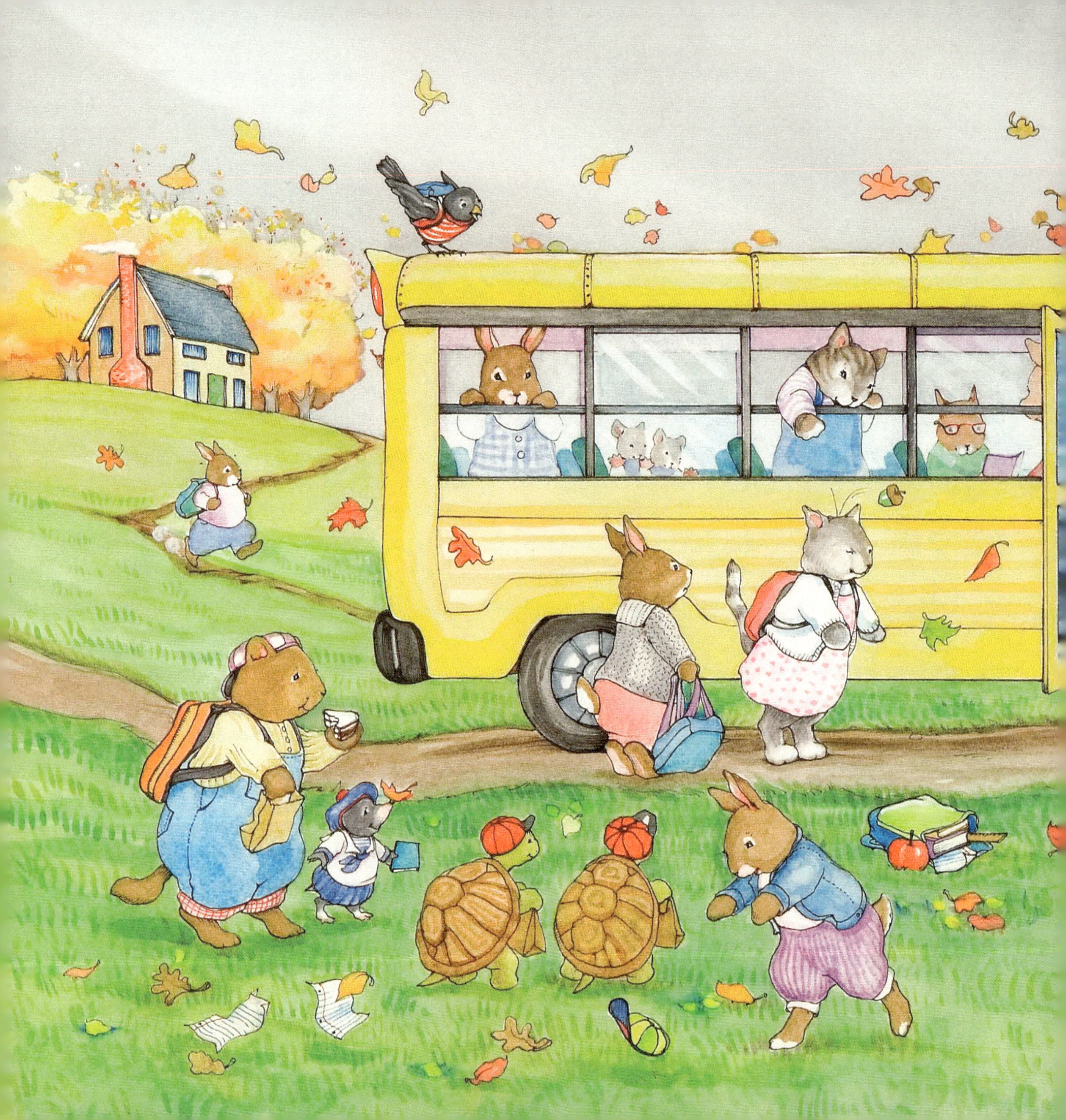

The blustery wind and the big yellow school bus know it's fall.

Flying footballs know it's fall.

Scurrying squirrels know it's fall.

What do you like about fall?

Who Knows it's Winter?

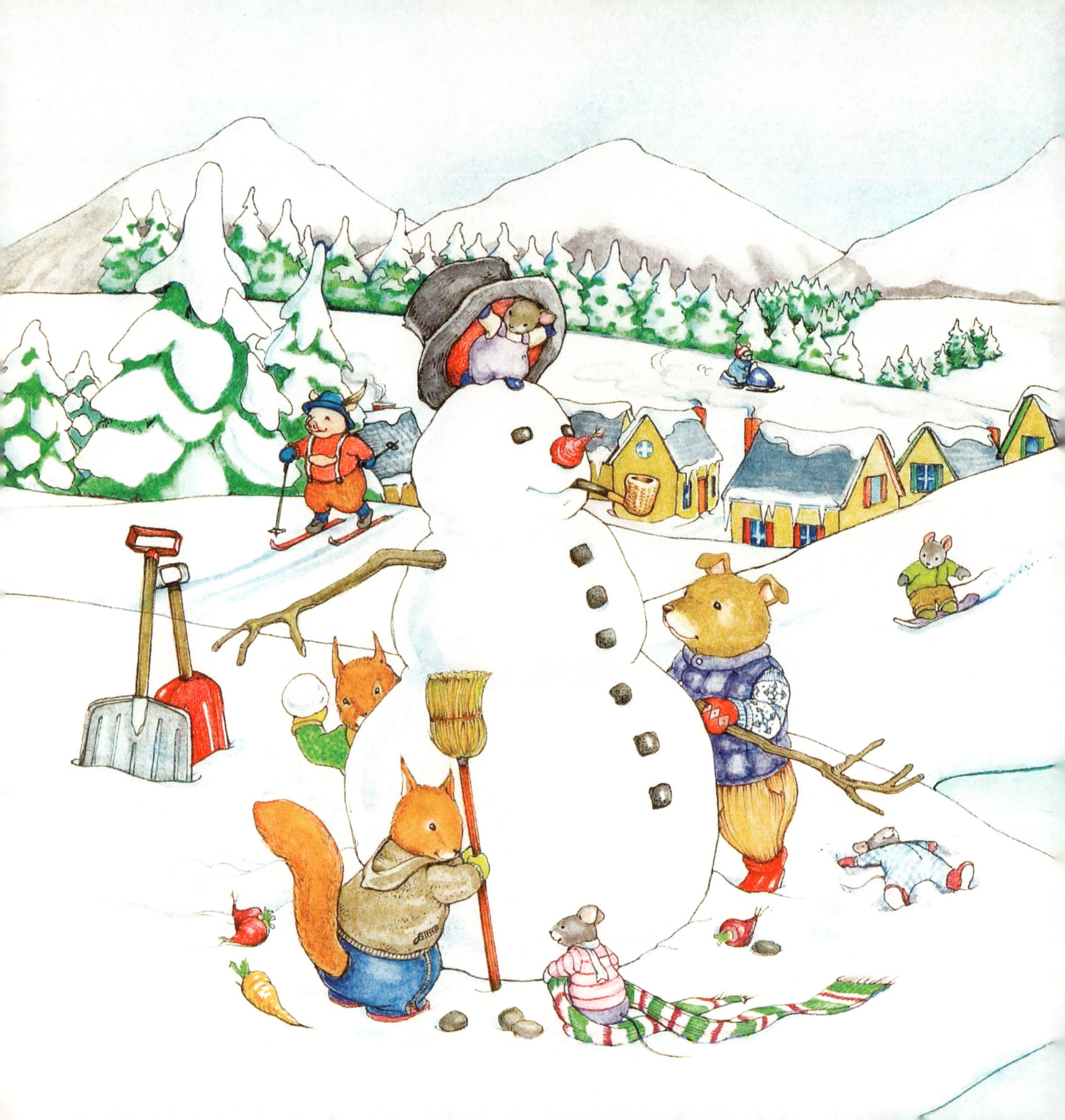

Jolly snowmen and spinning skaters know it's winter.

Dancing snowflakes know it's winter.

Bears, snug and snoozing, know it's winter.

What do you like about winter?

Who knows the seasons?

We know
the seasons!

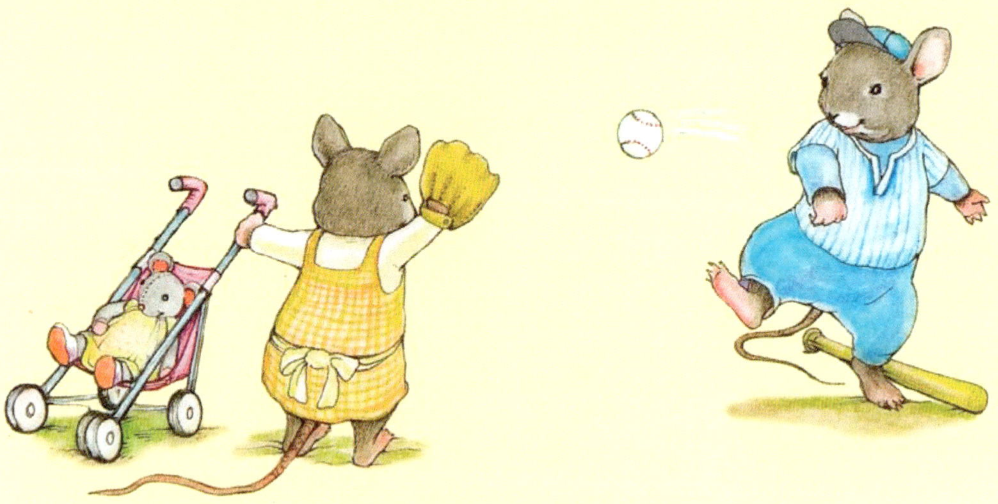